info buzz

David Attenborough

Stephen White-Thomson

W

FRANKLIN WATTS
LONDON • SYDNEY

Franklin Watts
First published in Great Britain in 2020 by The Watts Publishing Group
Copyright © The Watts Publishing Group, 2020

 Produced for Franklin Watts by
White-Thomson Publishing Ltd
www.wtpub.co.uk

Credits
Series Editor: Izzi Howell
Book Editor: Stephen White-Thomson
Series Designer: Rocket Design (East Anglia) Ltd
Designer: Clare Nicholas
Literacy Consultant: Kate Ruttle

The publisher would like to thank the following for permission to reproduce their pictures: Alamy: Keystone Press 10; Getty: Popperfoto 8, Popperfoto 9, David Cairns/Express 11; Nature Picture Library: Miles Barton cover and 4, Neil Lucas 5, John Sparks 13, Neil Nightingale 14, Huw Cordey title page, 17, Jordi Chias 19; Shutterstock: stok fotograf 7, Kurit Afshen 12 and 22, eventh 15, Efimova Anna 16, Tomas Kotouc 18, Himanshu Sharif 20, ASPARINGGA 21.

Every attempt has been made to clear copyright. Should there be any inadvertent omission please apply to the publisher for rectification.

Printed in Dubai

Franklin Watts
An imprint of
Hachette Children's Group
Part of The Watts Publishing Group
Carmelite House
50 Victoria Embankment
London EC4Y 0DZ

An Hachette UK Company
www.hachette.co.uk
www.franklinwatts.co.uk

All words in **bold** appear in the glossary on page 23.

Contents

Who is David Attenborough?

David Attenborough is a British **naturalist** and **broadcaster**. He is very interested in all the creatures that live on planet Earth.

▲
David with a golden eagle in his film, *The Life of Birds* (1998).

David tells stories about many different plants, animals and insects – big and small. He writes books and makes **documentaries** for us to watch.

David is filmed on an Indian elephant in *The Life of Mammals* (2002). ▼

What is the most interesting animal that you've met?

Childhood

David was born on 8 May 1926 in London, **UK**. His family moved to Leicester when his father became head of the university.

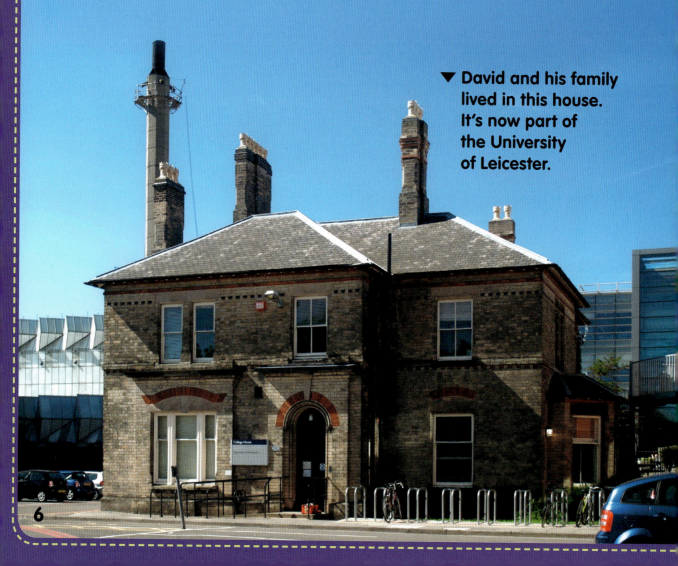

▼ David and his family lived in this house. It's now part of the University of Leicester.

As a child, David collected old birds' eggs that had fallen to the ground. He also found **fossils**. He kept them in a little **museum** he made in his home.

▼ David enjoyed watching newts in a nearby pond.

Have you seen creatures in a pond near you?

Joining the BBC

David studied **natural sciences** at university. In 1950, he married Jane Oriel. They had two children, Susan and Robert.

◄ David with his children – and pet cat!

In 1952, David joined the **BBC**. At the time, the BBC was the only television (TV) station in the UK. All the **programmes** shown were in black and white. At first, David didn't even have a TV at home.

◀ This is one of the first TV cameras that the BBC used to film their programmes.

Working for the BBC

David soon started to **present** TV programmes. He wanted to share his interest in the natural world with his TV **audience**.

David showed Cocky the Cockatoo to a young Prince Charles and Princess Anne. ▼

In 1965, David became head of BBC Two. In 1968, he was made the Director of Programmes for BBC One and BBC Two. Around now, it became possible to watch TV in colour.

◀ This is David at the time he was made head of BBC Two.

Life on Earth

In 1972, David left the BBC to write and make his own films. In 1977, *Life on Earth* was broadcast.

◀ David filmed some amazing creatures, like this rainforest frog.

Life on Earth was watched by more than 500 million people in nearly 100 countries! A big team of people helped David to make the programme.

▼ In a scene from *Life on Earth,* David briefly became part of this gorilla family!

How do you think David felt at this moment?

Plants and birds

People enjoyed *Life on Earth* so much that David wrote and presented more *Life* programmes. One of these was *The Private Life of Plants* (1995). It showed plants from all around the world.

◀ David looked up at a huge cactus plant growing in the Sonoran Desert in the United States of America.

In *The Life of Birds*, David was amazed to see how birds, like hornbills, behaved. *Life in the Freezer* showed how birds, and other creatures, lived in very cold places.

In *Life in the Freezer* (1993), we learned about the lives of king penguins in Antarctica. ▼

Mammals

David travelled all over the world to make *The Life of Mammals* (2002). He used special cameras to show how lions behaved at night.

Elephants were one of many mammals that featured in the film. ▼

David and his film crews worked very hard to take the most exciting shots. David liked to get as close as he could to the animals in his films.

Would you like a job like David's? Why?

David watched how meerkats behaved during the filming of *The Life of Mammals*. ▼

Life in the oceans

David has presented two big documentaries about the oceans: *Blue Planet* (2001) and *Blue Planet 2* (2017).

What would it feel like to swim with a whale?

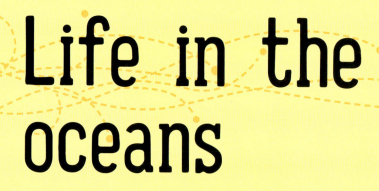

A humpback calf (baby) swims just below the surface of the water. ▶

David's films show us that we
need to change the way we live.
Plastics and other **pollution**
harm sea creatures and **coral**.

▲ Fish need
heathy coral
to survive.

Protecting the planet

Recently, David has spoken out more about the dangers of **climate change**. Humans need to understand how things they do can harm animals, plants and insects.

Global warming is harming the **habitats** of many creatures, including **polar bears**. ▶

David has spent his life filming creatures all over the Earth. He wants us to take care of all of them, from tiny butterflies to giant whales.

◄ The planet we live on is beautiful. We need to look after it.

Quiz

Test how much you remember.

Check your answers on page 24.

1 Where was David Attenborough born?

2 What did David study at university?

3 When was David made head of BBC Two?

4 How many people watched *Life on Earth*?

5 Name one of the birds filmed in *Life in the Freezer*.

6 Name an animal harmed by global warming.

Glossary

audience – all the people who watch or listen to a play, a film, a TV or a radio programme

BBC – British Broadcasting Corporation produces and broadcasts TV and radio programmes

broadcaster – a person or organisation that sends something out as a television or radio programme

climate change – climate is the sort of weather that a place has; the world's climate is changing quickly

cockatoo – a large type of parrot

coral – a type of rock that is made in the sea from the bodies of tiny creatures

documentary – a film or TV programme that presents the facts about a person or event

fossils – parts of dead plants or animals that have been in the ground for millions of years and have turned to stone

global warming – the process by which the Earth is getting warmer because of pollution in the atmosphere

habitats – the places where animals or plants usually live and grow

mammal – an animal that gives birth to live babies and feeds its young with its own milk

museum – a place where special things are kept for people to see

naturalist – a person who studies nature, especially plants and animals

natural sciences – study of plants and animals and their habitats

newt – a small creature that often lives on land but lays eggs in water

pollution – when air or water is made dirty

present – introduce a show

programme – a show on the radio or television

rainforest – a large forest in warm parts of the world where there is a lot or rain

UK – The United Kingdom is a group of countries made up of England, Wales, Scotland and Northern Ireland

Index

Answers:

1: London, UK; 2: Natural sciences; 3: 1965; 4: 500 million; 5: King penguins; 6: Polar bears

Teaching notes:

Children who are reading Book Band Gold or above should be able to enjoy this book with some independence. Other children will need more support.

Before you share the book:

- Have children heard of David Attenborough? What do they know about him?
- Explain that Attenborough makes films about plants and animals. Which plants and animals would the children like to learn more about?

While you share the book:

- Help children to read some of the more unfamiliar words.
- Talk about the questions. Encourage children to make links between their own experiences and Attenborough's.

- Discuss the information about Attenborough's early life. How did this affect his adult life?
- Talk about the wildlife pictures. Ask children in which environments they think they were taken.

After you have shared the book:

- Talk about the different jobs people do to make TV films. Which jobs would children like to do?
- Share clips of some of David Attenborough animal encounters. Talk about why his work is important.
- Work through the free activity sheets at www.hachetteschools.co.uk

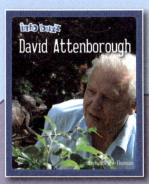

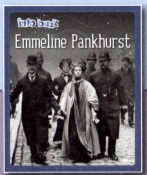

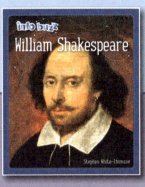

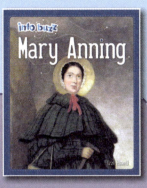

History

People who help us

Countries

Religion

STEM

Franklin
WATTS